The Hedgecraft Kitchen

Over 70 recepies for health, hearth and home.

Tamlin J. McPherson

Sweets and Lozenges

Lozenge recipes
SORE THROAT LOZENGE
COUGH DROPS
SETTLER SWEETS
BREATH OF AIR
DIAREASE
DAMBUSTER SWEETS
MINTY BECALMERS
BECALMERS
TRAVEL SWEETS
SKULLSEASE

Teas

Tea recipes
SLEEPY TEA
MONTHLY TEA
HANGOVER TEA
HAYFEVER TEA
SETTLING TEA
COFFIN' TEA
PICK ME UP
FLU TEA
HEARTY TEA

Herb Mixes & Incense

Incense recipes
SLEEPY INCENSE
WAKE UP INCENSE
CONCENTRATION INCENSE
MOOD LIFT INCENSE
TRANQUILITY INCENSE
BUG FREE INCENSE
PARTY INCENSE
CLENSING INCENSE
PASSION INCENSE
FEARLESS INCENSE

Around the Home.

Herb and Fruit wines.

Herb guide

A note on contents..
While yes this is reference book, I want to try and engage the reader and encourage them to read through this book, I would dread to think that a person only ever turns to a particular page as they might miss a valuable little gem of a recipe they haven't seen before, with this in mind I have removed all page numbers, go forth, explore, flick backwards and forwards, and to hell with conventions!

Preface

Everywhere I turn these days, I see fad diets; get healthy quick schemes and endless convenience pills guaranteed to cure the thing that ails you, or some horrible chemical in a non recyclable spray bottle that promises to unnecessarily sanitise your world, all the while funding large businesses that don't care who they trample on as long as they can keep pimping their toxic rubbish in to the high street shops.

I have written this book in hope that you take a little knowledge and a lot of self awareness away with you, in hope that you will take away a few of my favourite recipes for household items people have been wasting money on for too long.

Further to the household recipes I have included some of my tried and tested treatments for the all too common ailments people are so fond of running to the pharmacy to treat, when the treatments are probably on your doorstep!

In this book you will find several recipes for common household items and treatments for various ailments. In reference to the treatments, some will have different recipes for the same ailment, depending on how you prefer to administer them.

You will find that some recipes will hide some of the less pleasant tastes and smells of some herbs, and others won't. Because we're using natural herbs, you can expect to run the gamut of smells and tastes, so I have provided differing recipes for differing pallets.

Introduction

Chemicals, when that word is spoken or seen what do people conjure up with it? To my mind it's usually the image of large pharmaceutical companies dumping hazardous substances in to the environment or the "recreational" drugs we see on the television and hear about on the radio.
For me it inspires images of the junkie, the dealer and the large pharmacological companies who only think of selfish profit instead of the world they rape to get their profit margin.

Perhaps it makes you think of scientific health, of bleached clean laboratories and men in white coats peering in to microscopes, trying to dissect a chemical at an atomic level to extract the latest convenience to reach the pharmacist shelves or worse still, the vivisection performed on animals in the name of progressing medical or cosmetic science. In either case, it's not a comfortable image to sit with and certainly not something I want done in my name.

This book then is aimed at people who want another option that works and isn't going to harm ourselves, others or the environment we live in. You will find the recipes in this book split in to several sections, complete with a no nonsense general "how to" at the beginning of each section, and step by step instructions on how to prepare each treatment. Later on in the book I have included a small herb guide, It isn't by any means exhaustive and only includes the herbs and plants I have used in this book, so you can get out there and hunt around the hedgerows for yourself to find the herb ingredients you need.

A note on herbs, I would like to think that you would be adventurous enough to go out and find the herbs you need, unfortunately we can't all live in the countryside and sometimes a person has to rely on shops for their herbal supplies. Should you be one of these people, what I will say is there are many reputable retailers of herbs, and with a few careful questions you will be able to find a good supplier.

Try in all cases to find one which will sell the herbs dried and chopped by weight, not pre packed, so you may buy as much or as little as you need. Make sure that the dried herbs aren't too old, as the active constituents in them will have all but died off if they are too old.

Try to ascertain where the herbs are from. Were they grown in the UK, Europe or abroad? Were they grown organically, were they grown without pesticides? Asking a few questions before you make a purchase is a worthwhile activity, it's something a reputable retailer won't object to and will help you to be confident in using the herbs you buy. Further to this, If you intend to make the creams, be very careful about the base you use, the best is beeswax, and you'll find initially beeswax isn't easy to come by, but by making a quick call to your local beekeeping group (most of which have some kind of internet presence) they should put you in contact with a beeswax supplier, and from there, you will be able to create the most wonderful creams.

In all cases where you are making a herbal treatment which involves other ingredients, try to go for the better quality, organic produce, you will find the reward for procuring these items is more than just the quality of the item, but also in the knowledge that by doing so, you are contributing to good farming and fair -trading practice.

Home Made Essential Oils – Oil Infusion

"Unleaded or diesel?"

OK, as you'll be using oils within some of these recipes, it makes sense to provide you with a how to for making your own, now we're not suggesting you distill entire fields full of herbs to create a super concentrated essential oil, as that is costly, tricky and potentially dangerous! I don't want anyone buying a small distillery just to make normal essential oil.

The method I refer to is a much simpler method, and is probably better referred to as an infusion of oil rather than essential oil, but this method does leach the essential oils from the plants and herbs, and does create essential oil, just not the kind you'd buy in a shop.

There are two methods to making oils, one for the summer and one for the winter or in emergencies.

So what will you need is for the summer method is:
Clear glass jars with wide openings (Jam jars) and re-sealable lids.
A series of brown glass "eye dropper" jars, the same used in Bach flower remedies. (You can get these at most herbalist shops or chemists.)
A small piece of muslin, undyed cotton or other porous natural non dyed fabric.
A glass measuring jug.
Sticky labels.
Olive oil.
Herbs.
Patience!!

How to make essential oil – summer method

Prepare the herbs you need by drying and chopping them; you will need 1 ounce of herbs for every 8 fluid ounces of oil. Once chopped place the herbs in to the jar and cover in the oil. It is important that the herbs you place in to the oil have been thoroughly dried and they have no water within them as the liquid within the plant can harbour bacteria which can be harmful to you, and that's the last thing you want!

Place the oil on a sun facing window ledge and shake vigorously daily. After one week has passed place a piece of muslin over your measuring jug and strain the oil in to the jug, squeeze the muslin to get all the oil out of the herbs, then replace the old herbs for new ones and pour the oil back in to it. Place it back on to the window ledge and start the process again.

This needs to be done at least for at least one week , but two weeks is better, naturally, the longer you this, the stronger the concentration of oil.

When the oil is ready, strain through muslin once more in to the measuring jug and label up your dropper bottles, then pour the resulting oil infusion in to your dropper bottles. Stored in a cool dry area these will keep for up to 12/18 months, after which, their vitality wanes

What you need for the winter method:
A largish sauce pan.
Clear glass jars with wide openings (Jam jars) and resalable lids.
A series of brown glass "eye dropper" jars, the same used in Bach flower remedies. (You can get these at most herbalist shops or chemists.)
A small piece of muslin, undyed cotton or other porous natural non dyed fabric.
A glass measuring jug.
Sticky labels.
Olive oil.
Herbs.

How to make essential oil infusions – winter/emergency method

First, you'll need to mix the oil and herbs together, heating them up in a largish pan with the lid on, on low heat for about 6 hours (you do not want to heat the oil too high, you're not cooking the herbs! As warm as a bath is about right, you can do this in the oven, if it will go low enough). Once it has sat in heated oil for 6 hours, the liquid needs to be strained with muslin cloth. Pour this in to your measuring jug and from there in to your labeled dropper. These oils will last approximately 6 months if kept in a cool dark place.

Tinctures

"A wee nip of what you fancy"

I've started with tinctures as they are the easiest treatment to make, and the simplest to take. The only thing you need to bear in mind is the amount of time it takes to prepare a tincture, so it's not really suitable for instant treatment and is better that you make them as the seasons change, so you have them in stock for when you start to feel under the weather. For more instant treatment, take a look at the section called "Teas".

To make these tinctures you're going to need:
A bottle over either over proof rum or
A bottle of navy strength Plymouth Gin or
Any alcohol made for normal consumption which is over 50% abv.
A few small wide topped jars, jam jars are perfect.
A series of brown glass "eye dropper" jars, the same used in Bach flower remedies. (You can get these at most herbalist shops or chemists.)
A small piece of muslin, undyed cotton or other porous natural non dyed fabric.
A glass measuring jug.
Sticky labels.

How to make a tincture

Collect the herbs you require, whether that be from a local herbalist shop or your nearby hedgerow, make sure that you prepare the herbs correctly (if you bought them from a herb shop, they will already be prepared) if you have picked them from your local environment, make sure they are washed and have no bugs on them (extra protein! Seriously though, we don't want to kill them, and we don't want to spoil the tincture) chop them up finely and add the measured amount given in the recipe in to the jam jar.

Open up the alcohol and pour enough to completely cover the herbs, put the lid on the jam jar to seal it. Place them somewhere dark and room temperature, you'll need to check on them daily and give them a brief shake.

After a minimum of 4 weeks the alcohol will begin to discolour, as the chemical compounds of the herbs leech in to the alcohol, if you can leave it for up to 8 weeks, great! If not then 4 weeks really is the minimum time to leave them.

Recover your jars and take a glass measuring jug, cover the top of the measuring jug in muslin or another clean non coloured porous fabric and slowly pour the liquid from the jam jar in to the measuring jug. When the liquid has poured, scoop out the herbs in to the cloth and close it up around the herbs, squeeze the bag until all the moisture comes out of the herbs.

Take the resulting liquid (which should be a lot less than the amount you began with) and carefully pour it in to the eye dropper jars, not forgetting to label them up with the contents and the date you made them.

Always take a tincture diluted in to another drink, it will mix with alcohol best, but it can be taken with fruit juice or water, they are not intended to be taken without dilution as they are pure alcohol, and pure alcohol can be unpleasant on the tongue!

Tincture recipes

PICK ME UP
½ Echinacea
½ Goldenseal

Perfect for boosting your immune system when you're feeling a bit under the weather, great for helping fight off infections, fevers and viruses.
Take 10 to 15 drops diluted up to three times per day.

ASTHMA RELIEF
½ Mullein
½ Purslane

Works by helping to open the airways and increase lung capacity.
Take as part of your standard treatment not as a replacement to it.
Take 10 drops diluted in a drink as a compliment to your standard treatment.

COUGH TREATMENT
½ Horehound
½ Coltsfoot

This simple tincture can be used to bring relief to coughs by easing the reflux of the lungs and calming the soreness in the throat.
Take 15 to 20 drops diluted up to four times per day

CALMING TINCTURE
½ St. Johns Wort
½ Lemon Balm

This old recipe is one of my favourites, as it is a great treatment against panic and anxiety; it also functions to calm the nervous system and can be taken regularly as an anti depressant.
Take 10 drops diluted 2 twice a day, or as needed when you feel moments of panic.

SLEEPY TINCTURE
2 parts Valerian
1 part Hops
1 part Chamomile (German)

Once referred to as knockout drops by a friend, this treatment is very effective at helping you get a good night's sleep. It is best taken diluted with an alcoholic nightcap about 20 minutes before bedtime.
Take 20 drops diluted within 30 minutes before you go to bed.

HEADACHE HELP
2 parts White Willow Bark
1 part Chamomile (German)
2 parts Feverfew
1 part Peppermint

Another old recipe taught to me many years ago, it's great to take together with the Hangover tea to deliver a double whammy.
Place 15 to 20 drops in to your dilute, up to 3 times a day.

HAYFEVER TINCTURE
2 parts Nettle
1 part Yarrow
2 parts Chamomile (German)

I once had a friend who suffered terribly with all manner of allergies to fur, hair and hay fever, initially the allergy tea served him well, but this tincture will give longer term help against the issues of allergies and hay fever.
Take 20 drops in a dilute as often as you need to.

REGULAR TINCTURE 1
½ Marsh Mallow
½ Dandelion Root

I remember Dandelion root being used in tea as a child as a treatment against constipation, and as I have grown have discovered this recipe blended as a tincture can bring great relief.
Add 15 drops to your dilute up to three times per day.

REGULAR TINCTURE 2
1 part Fennel
2 parts Ginger
2 parts Cinnamon

Unfortunately, constipation isn't the only problem one can face, and for those times when diarrhoea becomes a problem, this will help to clear that up.
Take 20 drops added to a dilution up to three times per day.

MUSCLE EASE
2 parts Chamomile
1 part Lemon Balm

This gentle tincture will help to ease the aches and pains of a day in the garden, or the gym!

Creams

"Single, double or whipped?"

The soothing touch of a cream on conditions like eczema can produce one of the most rewarding looks of gratitude a herbalist can get from someone who applies it for the first time. The strangest thing is a natural cream is so easy to make, I'm surprised that more people don't do it. When you make creams you can use cocoa butter or beeswax, and it's best to use these interchangeably for people who may be allergic to chocolate (gods forbid!) or suffer from the allergic reaction to bee stings and don't want to take the chance. In either case the recipe is fairly simple and you will find you have everything you need already in the kitchen.

To make creams you will need:
Herbs/flowers.
Enough water to cover the herbs/flowers.
1oz Beeswax (adjust the amount to make more or less, as required.)
Small pan.
A medium sized bowl.
Pestle & mortar or a bowl and a rolling pin end.
4oz vegetable oil or olive oil.
2oz water.
Water for boiling.
Double boiler (a bowl on top of boiling water in a pan so you can melt stuff in the bowl as you would melt chocolate).
A strainer.
A whisk (hand or motorised).
Small sealable pots.
Sticky labels.

How to make creams

Take the herbs or flowers that you need and bruise them in your pestle & mortar (or equivalent), once bruised, place the mixture in to a small pan, add enough water to just cover them, place a lid on the top and bring to the boil. Once boiled allow it to cool to a simmer and allow to simmer for ten to fifteen minutes, and then let it cool. Using a sieve or strainer strain the liquid in to a bowl and place in to a refrigerator for a few hours (if using an oil instead you can skip the above process and move straight to the below section).

Take your double boiler and make sure the water in the bottom of the pan is on a fast simmer, place the beeswax or cocoa butter in the bowl above it and melt them to a soft texture. Stir in to this a few tablespoons of vegetable or olive oil (olive oil is better quality, you will need to adjust the amount of olive oil you add depending on the consistency of cream you want, the more you add, the more liquid the cream will be, you'll have to experiment to get the consistency you want.) slowly, a bit at a time then remove it from the heat and begin to whisk it adding the cool herb water (or oils). When thoroughly mixed it should be the consistency of very soft wax. Put the mixture in to your sealable pots and label them. Keep them refrigerated and they will keep for a few months.

A note on measurements, where I refer up "cups" I am not referring to an American measurement, I literally mean "a cup", it seems the simplest way to generalise the measurements and allows you to increase or decrease your proportions and keeps the balance of ingredients correct. Also, the oil measurements might seem high, this is because this refers to oils you have made as I have described in this book, if you are using distilled essential oils, halve these measurements.

Cream recipes

SUNBURN CREAM
40 drops Lavender oil
30 drops Tea Tree oil
30 drops Aloe Vera gel

This soothing cream will aid with the irritation and itch of sunburn, of course, prevention is better than cure, and in hind sight everyone uses sun cream, but for those occasions when you are caught out by the sun, this will help to soothe the pain of sunburn.

EYE CREAM
½ cup fresh Violet flowers
½ cup fresh Violet leaves
40 drops Echinacea oil
40 drops Chamomile oil (optional)

Mix as described, apply around the lids and the bags of the eyes to refresh and tighten the skin.

DEODERANT BAR (SOLID CREAM)
60 drops Thyme oil
60 drops Rosemary oil
50 drops Lavender oil
3 drops Castor oil

Melt beeswax in a glass jar standing in hot water, when it has melted, add the oils. Stir to mix thoroughly, then pour into a clean mould and leave to cool and set for a more solid bar, increase the amount of beeswax).

SKIN CREAM
3 tablespoons dried Lemon Balm leaves
2 teaspoons Lemon juice
30 drops Lavender oil
1 teaspoon Aloe Vera gel

Mix as described, this citrus smelling skin cream will help to tone and moisturise your skin.

ACNE CREAM
3 teaspoons Lemon juice
40 drops Tea Tree oil
20 drops Mint

Apply this cream daily to speed up the process of clearing spots from the skin, works especially well with the skin cream when used daily.

WOUND CREAM
½ cup Aloe Vera leaf
½ cup Calendula
¼ cup Chickweed
½ cup Marshmallow
30 drops Tea Tree oil

Mix given the directions above, this soothing antiseptic, anti-inflammatory cream will help to heal bumps, cuts and grazes and rashes of the skin.

ECZEMA CREAM
¼ cup Aloe Vera leaf
¼ cup Calendula
¼ cup Liquorice
¼ cup Burdock
30 drops Tea Tree oil

Prepare this cream as described and apply to the affected area for relief from the symptoms of eczema

BRUISE CREAM
½ cup Calendula
½ cup Witch Hazel
1 cup Arnica

This old recipe is the best treatment I know of for treating bruises, it deals with the swelling, the discolouration and the pain.

STING SALVE
1 cup Feverfew
1 cup Comfrey
1 cup Goldenseal
30 drops Chamomile oil

This soothing slave will help to take away the redness and itching from nettle stings and other simple skin rashes –

please note if a rash persists you must always seek the advice of a doctor.

SHAVING CREAM GEL
½ cup Aloe Vera gel*
3 teaspoons (1 tablespoon) Beeswax
20 drops Calendula oil
20 drops Comfrey oil
10 drops Lavender oil
5 drops Peppermint oil

*Aloe Vera Gel is obtained by taking a few stout leaves of the Aloe Vera plant and cutting the end off and squeezing the gel straight out of the leaf, ½ a cup sounds like a lot, but three or four leaves should give you the amount you need.

Mix the beeswax and oils as mentioned above. Just after you have added the oils and are stirring the mix add the Aloe Vera gel until you have a smooth cream.

Store in a sealed container and keep chilled, when chilled should keep for a few weeks.

NATURAL SHAMPOO
2 cups Water
2 ½ tablespoons Soapwort root, chopped
1 teaspoon Lemon juice
1 teaspoon Lemon Verbena, dried and chopped
1 teaspoon Mint dried and chopped.
Unlike the creams thus far, this is a liquid. Do not follow the directions given above, instead, follow the following instructions.

Soak the soapwort overnight in the water then boil the soapwort in the water for around 30 minutes with the lemon verbena and mint, then strain through muslin or other non-dyed porous material. Pour in to a suitable bottle and keep refrigerated, will keep for approx 1 to 2 weeks.

WORKOUT CREAM
2 cups Chamomile (Roman)
1 cup Arnica
½ Lemon Balm

This light cream applied to aching muscles will help to sooth the pains of a hard day's work, or a hard day's workout!

Sweets and Lozenges

"Sugar and spice and all things nice"

Lozenges are one of the nicest ways to take herbal treatments, although you will need to remember they aren't just sweeties! I have found that lozenges are the best way to administer treatments to children with the sniffles.

To make Lozenges you will need:
Powdered herbs.
Oils or essential oils.
Honey.
Icing sugar.
Rolling pin.
Wooden spoon.
Sharp knife.
Mixing bowl.

How to make a lozenge

There are a number of different ways a person can make herbal sweets, the most effective is to add drops of a tincture to the recipe, however if you don't have the tincture to hand, oils or powdered (not just finely chopped, powdered) herb added as below will do.

Mix your herbs and / or oils together and then add enough honey to make a thick, gooey mass. It takes less honey than you'd think so start out slowly with the honey. When using essential oils always make sure they are safe for internal consumption as some can be quite strong.

Roll the mass in icing sugar to coat and then roll out until about ¼ inch thick. Cut the dough into one inch pieces, roll them into a ball and place on a cooling rack flattening them as you are doing this (making them in to a disc shape). Set out to dry for about 12 hours then store them in a labeled airtight jar when dry.

Lozenge recipes

SORE THROAT LOZENGE
3 tbsp powdered Slippery Elm bark
3 tbsp powdered Liquorice root
1 tbsp powdered Echinacea root and leaf
1 tsp powdered Wild Cherry bark

Prepare as described above, enjoy after a night out cheering at a gig, or just when your throat isn't at it's best.

COUGH DROPS
2 tbsp powdered Marshmallow
2 tbsp powdered Rosemary
1 tbsp powdered Thyme
1 tsp powdered Elderberries

These make lovely purple lozenges that sooth a cough, aiding sleep.

SETTLER SWEETS
4 tbsp powdered Peppermint
3 tbsp powdered Chamomile
2 tbsp powdered Raspberry leaf

This lovely minty sweet will help to ease an upset stomach.

BREATH OF AIR
4tbsp powdered Peppermint
4tbsp powdered Spearmint
3tbsp powdered Lemon Balm
2tbsp powdered Lemon Verbena

This powerful lozenge will help to blow away the cobwebs and clear out the sinuses

MOTHERS SWEETS
4tbsp powdered Yarrow
3tbsp powdered Raspberry leaf
2tbsp powdered Meadowsweet
1tsp powdered Ginger

These spicy little gems will help to ease the pain that each woman gets at that time of the month.

DIAREASE
4tbsp powdered Agrimony
3tbsp powdered Bilberries/Blueberries (dried berries)
2 tbsp powdered Raspberry leaf

This lovely fruity sweet will aid in ridding the bowels of loose stools, and will help to get to back on your "regular" track.

DAMBUSTER SWEETS
4tbsp powdered Dandelion root
3tbsp powdered Raspberry leaf
1tbsp powdered Liquorice

Not getting enough fibre? Of course the best way to avoid constipation is to make sure you're getting enough fibre in your diet, however on those occasions where your movement is slowed, these little sweets will help to get you moving again!

MINTY BECALMERS
5 tbsp powdered Peppermint
4tbsp powdered Spearmint

These minty little starts help to relieve you of those occasions when flatulence gets the better of you. Take as required for relief from flatulence.

BECALMERS
3tbsp powdered Anise seed
2tbsp powdered Caraway
1tbsp powdered Fennel seed

This variant of Minty Becalmers was created for those of you who aren't keen on minty flavours.

TRAVEL SWEETS
4tbsp powdered Ginger
2tbsp powdered Raspberry leaf

For that time when travelling makes you feel green around the gills, take some of these spicy ginger sweets to suck on and they will help to relieve the queasy feeling during the journey.

SKULLSEASE
4tbsp powdered Ginger
4btsp powdered Feverfew
2tbsp powdered Lemon Balm

Occasionally the stresses of life manifest in to a pounding headache, when that happens try these sweets to ease the pain.

Teas

"Cup of brown joy"

Tea, is there really a better way to relax? If there is I don't want to know, for me, tea is one of the simplest and greatest pleasures a person can imbibe, there is nothing I feel that quenches the thirst better than tea! I digress, for unfortunately, it isn't the standard cup of Earl Grey I refer to here, this is a darker brew made of a mix of medicinal leaves steeped with the pure purpose of treating what ails you.

I'm not going to teach you to suck eggs here; everyone knows how to make a good cup of tea. Here I will simply point out the correct practice for making a herbal tea,

To make herbal tea you will need:
A Teapot or
A tea strainer or
A tea infuser or
A tea ball.
Boiling water.
Enough herb to half fill the above.
A cup (well, duh).

How to make a herbal tea

Firstly make sure the water is on a rolling boil, either make sure the electric kettle turns itself off, or if you're old fashioned like me wait until the stove top kettle is whistling happily to itself.
If you're using a teapot, and intend to have more than one cup of herbal tea you will need to have one heaped teaspoon

of herb for every cup, plus one "for the pot", just to make sure there is enough to infuse the water properly, fill the pot with the boiling water.

If you're using an infuser, strainer, ball or other device, make sure to half fill it, to allow the tea to circulate, then put it in/on the cup and fill the cup with boiling water.

In both cases, leave the tea to infuse in the water for at least 15 minutes, it's important you leave it for this long so the water can extract the compounds from the herbs.

After at least 15 minutes, remove the infuser/strainer/ball and enjoy! In the case of a tea pot, place a tea strainer on the cup and pour the herbal tea in to the cup, making sure the herbs are caught in the strainer.

Tea recipes

SLEEPY TEA
1 part Valerian
2 parts Chamomile
2 parts Lavender
1 part Lemon Balm

Take the crushed herbs and prepare as described above. Drink fifteen to twenty minutes before your bedtime. There is a tincture variation of this recipe, which is a lot stronger and is great for use with insomnia.

MONTHLY TEA
2 parts Raspberry leaf
1 parts Yarrow
2 parts Mugwort
2 part Anise
1 part Basil
1 part Bergamot

If you're not keen on aniseed, remove it and change yarrow to 2 parts.
This sweet tasting drink has been known to bring relief for women when menstruation is proving to be painful. Take up to 3 cups per day during your period.

HANGOVER TEA
1 part Rosemary
2 parts Bay leaf
3 parts Basil
1 part Thyme

Depending on how far you pushed the boat out the night before, you will need to administer this regularly throughout the day, it will help to re-hydrate you and will help with the headache and upset stomach that so often follows a long night out "on the tiles".

HAYFEVER TEA
2 part Nettle
1 part Echinacea
1 part Elderflower
1 part Feverfew
Prepare this in readiness for your friend if they have allergies to things within your home (animal hair, fur, dust etc) or if you or a friend has hay fever and are planning on stepping out when the pollen is high. You will need to have a cup every four or five hours that they'll be exposed.

SETTLING TEA
2 parts Peppermint
1 part Bergamot
2 parts Chamomile
1 part Fennel
1 part Basil

Made for anyone who regularly gets motion sickness, this simple tea with ease the stomach from its travel induced acrobatics Prepare this tea a thirty minutes before you plan to travel, it will help to ease any nervousness and the convulsions of the stomach. It has a pleasant minty taste.

GASEOUS TEA
1 part Angelica
1 part Basil
2 parts Fennel
2 parts Chamomile

Just occasionally, everyone gets unexpected trapped wind, and unfortunately, it has to go somewhere, use this tea to help release trapped wind in a more comfortable, socially acceptable way than the traditional way. Make this tea as you begin to feel the tell tale bloated and uncomfortable feeling, then have 1 cup every four hours as needed.

COFFIN' TEA
1 part Angelica
2 part Anise
1 part Basil
2 part Liquorice
1 part Echinacea
This sweet dark tea works to aid with a sore throat, eases your cough and calms a headache, as well as working hard to boost your immune system, take no more than three cups per day though, as too much liquorice can cause headache and can be a laxative!

PICK ME UP
2 parts Peppermint
2 parts Lemon Balm
1 part Sage
1 Bay leaf per cup

This zesty minty tea will blow away those cobwebs and help you to focus on the job at hand!

FLU TEA
2 parts Elderflower
3 parts Ginger
1 part Peppermint
2 parts Yarrow
1 part Feverfew
1 part Echinacea

When that nose won't stop running, and you can't stop sneezing, for those times when you're shivering even when covered in blankets, this tea will help to blow out those sinuses and help you back on the road to recovery.
This stonker of a tea will taste of ginger, and will become stronger the further down the cup you get, best taken before bed this tea will raise your temperature and help those antibodies do what they do best.
Other things you can do to break a cold or flu is to make sure you get plenty of foods with onion and garlic in it; foods from the onion family are great for flushing out the flu!

HEARTY TEA
1 part Peppermint
1 part Rosemary
1 part Thyme

This tea can be mixed with any other tea or standard tea if you feel so inclined, and will help to increase the amount of antioxidants you take in to your diet, helping to potentially ward off heart disease and cancer. Take as desired.

Herb Mixes & Incense

"Smoke 'em if you got 'em"

In this section I want to step away from digestible treatments, and move to a slightly more mood enhancing treatment (and no, I'm not referring to getting high, if you want that, you've got the wrong author) the simple act of burning incense and the effect it can have on the way it makes you feel.

It really is playtime here, I'm going to list a bunch of herbs and how they smell as incense, then I'll supply a few recipe mixes which make me feel a certain way, but this is all about you! I want you to experiment with herb blends to find out what makes you feel relaxed after a hard day, what refreshes you, what invigorates you.

To make incense you will need:
Self lighting charcoal brick (NOT BBQ Charcoal).
Dried herbs.
Sharp knife.
Pestle & mortar or coffee grinder.
Censer or non flammable bowl that you don't mind ruining.

How to make herb mixes and incense

Take a selection of the dried herbs you wish to burn (if you have bought this from a herb shop you won't need to cut it up) and with a sharp knife finely cut the herb in to small sections, then put it in to the pestle & mortar or coffee grinder (you need to be aware if you use a coffee grinder for cutting and blending herbs that you might break the coffee grinder! On your own head be it!) and grind the herb to even finer pieces.

Once the mixture is fine enough for you, light the charcoal brick (which are available at most new age shops and online) You might need to wait a little while for the brick to light properly as it can take time for the brick to begin to glow gently, a word of caution, charcoal bricks become very hot very quickly, you can be burned by them and they can set fire to flammable materials, they should be treated with great care and treated as if you had an open flame in the area.

Once the brick is glowing hot in the bowl, sprinkle a little of your incense (just a little to begin with) on to the brick to see how it smells and how thick the smoke is, once you are happy with that, you can continue to periodically apply more to refresh it, be advised though, too much will set off smoke alarms!

Incense can be a great way to unwind after a particularly stressful day, or can be the thing to wake you up when you're feeling down or tired, experiment with care, and enjoy.

Incense recipes

SLEEPY INCENSE
1 part Sandalwood
1 part Chamomile
1 part Lavender

WAKE UP INCENSE
1 part Eucalyptus
1 part Spearmint or Peppermint
1 part Anise
2 parts Lemon rind (dried)

CONCENTRATION INCENSE
2 parts Rosemary
1 part Sage
1 Part Anise seed

MOOD LIFT INCENSE
2 parts Ginger
2 parts Fennel seed
1 part Cinnamon

TRANQUILITY INCENSE
3 parts Rosemary
2 parts Sage
2 parts Thyme
1 part Lavender

BUG FREE INCENSE
3 parts Citronella leaves
2 parts Lemon rind (dried)
2 parts Orange rind (dried)
2 parts Sage
1 part Mint

PARTY INCENSE
3 parts Lemon Balm
3 Parts Anise Seed
2 parts Ginger
2 parts Liquorice

CLENSING INCENSE
3 parts Rosemary
2 parts Sage
2 parts Lavender
1 part Fennel seed

PASSION INCENSE
2 parts Elderberries (dried)
2 parts Hawthorn berries (dried)
2 parts Juniper berries (dried)
1 part Ginger
1 part Anise seed

FEARLESS INCENSE
3 parts Sage
2 parts Anise
2 Parts Ginger
1 part Liquorice

Around the Home.

"But my home's not round...."

Herb recipes are not all about healing ailments, there are a lot of practical uses for herbs around the home, long before the creation of chemical cleaners and polishers there was a wide variety of natural recipes used and we'll look in to those recipes in the following pages.

It is my sincere hope that if you do nothing else with this book, you take something from this section and realise that even the smallest change when it comes to chemical based cleaners can make a huge impact on the long term health of the environment.

By doing something as simple as changing to a natural floor polish you instantly alter the amount of chemicals you send down the drain, which in turn means a cleaner and healthier environment for everyone. When you scale that up to every household in the UK changing from chemical cleaners to natural ones, you can begin to see the positive environmental impact it would have. This is why it's important for each person to "do their bit" when it comes to looking after our environment.

The recipes below will have some new ingredients you may not have seen before in this book, such as petroleum jelly, fear not! We won't be using chemicals and I'll be showing you how to make a natural version. On the occasions where I introduce new ingredients I will advise on the best place to get them, or the best way for you to make them.

You will find a lot of these recipes call for beeswax, again it's better to approach your local beekeepers society to get hold of beeswax, but if absolutely necessary, it can be bought online. Who knows, though meeting local beekeepers it might encourage you to keep bees, helping the environment further and reaping the wonderful harvest of honey, beeswax and propolis they produce.

This is where the format of the book will have to change, due to the diverse nature of the recipes I'm not able to write a list of equipment or a how to make them at the top of the section as I have done in previous sections, instead I will advise the equipment required in the method after the ingredients, just like an old style recipe book.

Household recipes

NON PETROLEUM JELLY

1 ounce (weight) Beeswax
1/2 cup Olive Oil

Melt the beeswax in a microwave or a double boiler. Stir in the olive oil. Remove the mixture from the heat and stir until cool; this makes a handy alternative to Vaseline. Non petroleum jelly is easy to make and it is an ingredient of many other products

SOLID PERFUME

3 parts Olive Oil
2 parts Beeswax
1 part scent (any essential / infused oil you like the smell of)

Melt all ingredients over double boiler until well mixed and integrated. Pour into containers and let cool.

CANDLE WICKS

Mullein stalks

The herb Mullein was used centuries ago to make wicks for candles. You will have to find the seeds for Mullen and grow them yourself. Mullein is a tall straight plant with a hard stem. When the plant is fully grown and ripe, cut and remove the hard outer stem. In the centre of the stem is a vegetable cord like substance. Remove the cords and twist carefully, tying at top and bottom, then hang with a small weight like a pebble attached to the bottom. You can plait several cords of Mullein together to make the thickness of wick you require. Leave to dry for a few weeks, then use in candles as normal.

THREE IN ONE SOLID FURNITURE POLISH

Equal portions of linseed oil, warmed beeswax and turpentine.

This, like some of the other recipes, can be experimented with for best results. Here, it is good to begin with small quantities, about a cup of each ingredient. The warmed materials should be carefully and thoroughly mixed together with a wooden stick, then pour into the usual wide mouthed storage jar. The final colour is usually a rich gold.

BEESWAX FURNITURE POLISH #2

55g (2oz) Beeswax
280ml (1/2 pint) Turpentine
7g (1/4oz) fragrance or essential oil of your choice

You'll basically need to very gently heat the turpentine and wax in a metal saucepan, taking care not to allow it to simmer or boil. Mix the ingredients together as the wax dissolves. Bear in mind that turpentine is a flammable material, and so the necessary precautions should be made beforehand. If you like the smells of polishes like orange oil furniture polish, then at this stage you can add in a drop of fragrance oil once the mixture starts to cool. You can then transfer the mixture into a jar or container with a lid. Leave to cool.

This cream polish can then be applied to the wood with a lint-free cloth, before being buffed. The initial smell of turpentine will diminish quickly after application.

These recipes are easily made at home, but you should always make sure to take sensible precautions when heating and transferring hot liquids. Always take care to remove animals or children from your work area.

FLOOR POLISH

½ Beeswax
½ Turpentine

Melt equal portions together for use on wooden floors.

LEATHER WATERPROOFING

4 oz. Beeswax
4 oz. Resin/Rosin (music stores carry)
1 pint Olive Oil

Melt the solids in the oil, and apply while warm.

WATERPROOF & LEATHER SOFTENER

1 oz. (weight) Beeswax
8 oz. (weight) Non petroleum jelly

Melt the ingredients in a microwave or double boiler. Brush the hot mixture onto the leather and allow it to penetrate. If possible, place the item in hot sun. Polish the leather with a cloth to remove excess waterproofing.

ARTHRITIS WAX TREATMENT

5 lbs Beeswax
2 cups Olive Oil

Warm wax treatments are approved by the Arthritis Foundation to help relieve sore, painful joints caused by arthritis. Wax treatments provide moist heat, increase blood circulation, and ease stiffness due to joint inflammation.

Melt ingredients in an oven set between 170 to 200 degrees F. Stir to mix the oil and wax.

Remove the mixture from the oven and allow it to cool until there is a film of cooled wax on the surface (about 125 degrees F). Test the wax to be sure it is very warm, but not uncomfortable.

The body part treated must be clean and dry. Dip the body part into the wax mixture and withdraw it. If the hand is being treated, keep the fingers apart. Do this a few more times until there is a thick coating of wax.

Return the body part to the wax and leave there (15 to 30 minutes) until the mixture cools.

Remove the body part and peel off the wax.

Save the wax in a closed container to use again. The treatment may be repeated. The mixture will melt more quickly now that the oil and wax are combined.

Herb and Fruit Wines.

"What's your poison?"

There is nothing that impresses the palette more than home made wine, it really is a joy to taste and there are so many ways to make the best of natures harvest I will include as many recipes that I have been made aware of, some I have sampled first hand, others I have learned from their reputation alone.
If you have never made homebrew before don't be afraid of it, I know it seems like daunting task, but with a little knowledge, effort and patience, you can reap great rewards from your own fruit wine come a lazy summer evening.

I'll start this section as previously with the equipment you'll need and a basic "how to" some details may vary with each recipe and I'll cover those details in the method for each recipe. I'll also include some terminology to help the complete novices out there. As always I've approached this with a view to the idea that a total novice could read this section, then give it a go with resulting success.

Terminology

Demijohn: A large bottle with a short neck and two small handles at the neck; sometimes encased in wickerwork

Corker: a device to thrust corks in to wine bottles, these come as lever based or floggers, the lever ones are less work intensive.

Hydrometer: A hydrometer is an instrument used to measure the specific gravity (or relative density) of liquids; that is, the ratio of the density of the liquid to the density of water. A hydrometer is usually made of glass and consists of a cylindrical stem and a bulb weighted with mercury or lead shot to make it float upright.

Gravity: the gravity of a wine, measured by the hydrometer should be between 990 (dry) and 1020 (sweet), more notes on this later though.

To make wine you will need:
Fermenting drum (large bucket with a sealable lid).
Siphon tube.
1 x 4.5 litre glass demijohn.
Demijohn cork & fermentation lock.
6 empty wine bottles.
Plastic wine stoppers / wine corks (unused).
Corker.
Thermometer (non mercury) (this is optional but recommended).
Hydrometer (this is optional, but recommended).
Campden tablets.
Muslin strainer.
Wine yeast.
Sugar.

This is a basic equipment list to make a maximum of 6 bottles of wine, some of the recipes below will be for making more than that and you'll need to adjust accordingly.

How to make fruit and herb wines

Once you have put the pulped fruit/ chopped herbs / juice into the fermenting container, add enough water to just cover the fruit. Boil up 2 teaspoons of tea (or 2 teabags) for every gallon of wine and add this to the fermenting container. Adding the tea adds tannin, which will vastly improve the taste of your wine and is essential if you want your wine to keep.

You also need to add sugar and yeast. Ideally you should use about 1 kilo of sugar for every gallon of wine, but do not add it all at once. The yeast will convert the sugar into alcohol, and once the alcohol content is high enough, it will kill off the yeast. If you have added a lot of sugar and the alcohol level kills off the yeast before all the sugar is converted, then you will end up with a sweet wine. If you don't add enough sugar and the yeast is killed off then you will have a dry wine. A wine hydrometer can tell you the specific gravity of your wine (how much sugar remains in the liquid) and therefore how much sugar to add to give you the desired sweetness.

Most fruits as mentioned have natural sugar in them and without adding extra sugar; these can be turned into a wine of about 4% to 6% volume alcohol. This is a low alcohol content and the wine will not keep for long, although it could be drunk young. Most home wine makers prefer to make a stronger wine of about 12% to 17%, so sugar is needed to bring the alcohol content up to a level high enough to store longer.

If you have a hydrometer, calculate the amount of sugar required to give you the sweetness of you wine require. If your hydrometer reads 990, then this will be a dry wine and you will need to add sugar if you want to sweeten it. If your hydrometer reads 1020 then it will be a sweet wine. You will need to use the hydrometer several times while your wine is fermenting to test whether you need to add more sugar. Ideally you should aim to use 1 kilo of sugar per gallon (4.5 litres) of wine. If you do not have a hydrometer, you will have to rely on guesswork and experience. If your wine is too sweet, you can use less sugar in the next batch. If it's too dry, then you can use more sugar in the next batch.

You can use special wine yeast from a home brew shop. Wine yeasts can be added straight into the fermenting bin, but it is better to start them off in some warm fruit juice (the juice from your fruit is ideal) and then add it to your fermenting container once the yeast is bubbling. Yeast is found naturally in the bloom of grapes, so you can create your own yeast by crushing a few grapes into some warm natural fruit juice. Orange juice works well. Once this is bubbling, add it to your fermenting bin.

Making the wine

Place your ingredients in to your fermenting drum, your drum will need a lid to cover but not be airtight. Add some of the sugar to the fermenting bin and stir it in very well until it has all dissolved. Then add your yeast and your wine should start fermenting. You should ideally keep the fermenting bin at around 21C, so keeping it in your living room should be fine. Wine will continue to ferment at lower and higher temperatures, so don't worry if you don't have room in your living room. Fit the lid (not too tightly, allow the gases to escape!) onto the fermenting bin and leave the wine to ferment for about 4 to 7 days. Every day, test your wine with the hydrometer and add more sugar if necessary, remembering to stir well to dissolve the sugar. You will need to stop adding sugar when the fermenting stops due to too much alcohol and hopefully the wine we be sweetened to suit your palate.

After a few days, you need to draw off the liquid into fermenting jars (demijohns), leaving the fruit pulp behind. The easiest way is to pour the liquid through a strainer or a sieve. 2 or 3 thicknesses of muslin will do the job just as well. Squeeze the juice out of the remaining pulp to get as much juice as possible from the fruit. Fill the fermenting jars to within a couple of inches of the top and fit a bung with an airlock. The bung and airlock will allow the gases produced by the fermenting to escape and prevent unwanted bacteria and insects attacking your wine. Leave your jars to continue fermenting, testing with the hydrometer and adding sugar as necessary. Again you can keep these jars in the living room to allow the wine to continue fermenting.

Racking
Your wine will appear cloudy due to the yeast in the wine. After about 3 months or so, the wine will begin to clear as the yeast settles to the bottom of the jar as sediment. Once cleared, you should siphon the wine from the jar into a second jar, being careful not to transfer the sediment. This is known as racking. Again, fit a bung and airlock and leave the wine to continue fermenting. Your wine will still contain some yeast, this will multiply and your wine will again turn cloudy. After about 3 months, the wine should have cleared again and you should rack the wine a second time. You can now bottle the wine.

Bottling
Before bottling, ensure that your wine has completely finished fermenting. If the wine continues to ferment in the sealed bottles, then the gases produced by the fermenting will cause the bottles to explode. The racking will help prevent continued fermentation by removing the yeast. You

can tell if the wine has finished fermenting by leaving it in the fermenting jar after the second racking and fitting a bung and airlock. If the wine turns cloudy, then there is still yeast in the wine and it is still fermenting. You can stop the fermenting by adding one crushed Campden tablet for every gallon of wine. If the wine is not fermenting, then bottle the wine and seal the bottles with airtight caps or corks. If using corks, store the bottles on their sides to keep the cork wet and stop it from shrinking.

Fruit & Herb wine recipes

BIRCH SAP WINE
1 gallon Birch sap
4 1/2 cups granulated sugar
2 Oranges or 1 Lemon, sliced thin
Campden tablets
1 package wine yeast

Place birch sap in your fermenting bin. Add sugar. Stir to dissolve. Add oranges or lemon. Let it sit overnight.
Next day, Specific Gravity should be 1.090 - 1.100. Stir in yeast. Stir daily for 5 to 6 days or until Specific Gravity is 1.040. Strain out fruit and squeeze as much juice out of it as you can. Siphon into demijons and add airlock.
For a dry wine, rack in three weeks, and every three months for one year then bottle.
For a sweet wine, rack at three weeks. Add 1/2 cup sugar dissolved in 1 cup wine. Stir gently, and place back into the demijon. Repeat process every six weeks until fermentation does not restart with the addition of sugar. Rack every three months until one year old then bottle.
The wine is best if you can refrain from drinking it for one full year from the date it was started.

To get the birch sap without killing the tree, find a well aged tree with a trunk about 12 inches in diameter, drill a hole about 2cm wide and 5cm deep in to the base of the tree, stake a stake with a "U" shape trough carved in to it and hammer it in to the hole, allowing the sap to drip down the trough.

Hang a bucket underneath it and place a muslin cloth over the top to prevent insects falling in.

Once you have the sap you need use another stake to fill the hole neatly, then cut the excess off the end of the stake to make it flush with the trunk.

BLUEBERRY WINE
4 to 5 cups Blueberries
5 cups granulated sugar
2 teaspoon acid blend
1/2 tsp pectic enzyme
1 teaspoon nutrients
2 Campden tablet
1 package wine yeast
Water

Crush the fruit. Add 12 cups of water and all other ingredients except the yeast. Stir well to dissolve sugar. Let it sit overnight.

Specific gravity should be between 1.090 and 1.095. Sprinkle yeast over the mixture and stir. Stir daily for five days.

Strain the must and squeeze the juice out. Siphon into the demijon, add water to make up volume and attach airlock.

For a dry wine, rack in three weeks, and every three months for one year then bottle.

For a sweet wine, rack at three weeks. Add 1/2 cup sugar dissolved in 1 cup wine. Stir gently, and place back into the demijon. Repeat process every six weeks until fermentation does not restart with the addition of sugar. Rack it every three months until one year old then bottle.

The wine is best if you can refrain from drinking it for one full year from the date it was started.

BLACKBERRY WINE

12 cups Blackberries, fresh
5 1/2 cups granulated sugar
1 teaspoon yeast nutrient
1 teaspoon acid blend
1 Campden tablet
1/2 teaspoon pectic enzyme
1 package wine yeast
1 gallon water

Do not use overripe or spoiled berries. Crush the berries and place in fermenting bin. Add water, sugar, nutrients, acid blend, and pectic enzyme and crushed Campden tablet. Stir well to dissolve sugar. Let it sit overnight.

Specific gravity should be between 1.090 and 1.095. Sprinkle yeast over the mixture and stir. Stir daily for five or six days, until specific gravity is 1.040.

Strain the must and squeeze out as much juice as you can from the fruit. Siphon into a demijon and place airlock.

For a dry wine, rack in three weeks, and every three months for one year. Then bottle.

For a sweet wine, rack at three weeks. Add 1/2 cup sugar dissolved in 1 cup wine. Stir gently, and place back into the demijon. Repeat process every six weeks until fermentation does not restart with the addition of sugar. Rack every three months until one year old then bottle.

The wine is best if you can refrain from drinking it for one full year from the date it was started.

CHERRY WINE
6 pounds Cherries
1 pound Raisins
5 cups granulated sugar
2 Campden tablets
1 teaspoon nutrients
3/4 teaspoon pectic enzyme
1 large Orange (juice only)
1 package wine yeast
Water

Crush the cherries. The goal here is the break the skin of every fruit to help the juice leach into the water, but not to damage the stones. Place them in the fermenting bin. Add enough cold water to cover. Stir in crushed Campden tablets and pectic enzyme. Let it sit for 2 days. Strain the fruit, squeezing out as much juice as possible. Add the balance of the ingredients (except yeast) and make up to 1 gallon with water. Check the specific gravity. It should be between 1.090 and 1.110. Add the yeast and mix in well. Cover the fermenting bin. Stir daily for three to five days, until frothing ceases.
Strain in to the demijon and attach an airlock.

For a dry wine, rack in three weeks and return to demijon. Rack again in three months, and every three months until 1 year old then bottle.

For a sweet wine, rack at three weeks. Add 1/2 cup sugar dissolved in 1 cup wine. Stir gently, and place back into the demijon. Repeat the process every six weeks until fermentation does not restart with the addition of sugar. Rack every three months until one year old then bottle.

This wine is best if you can refrain from drinking it for a year and a half from the date it was started.

DANDELION WINE
1 gallon Dandelion flowers, fresh
5 1/2 cups granulated sugar
1 teaspoon yeast nutrient
2 Oranges, juice and rind
2 Lemons, juice and rind
2 Campden tablets
1 package wine yeast
1 gallon water, boiling

Pinch off any green calyces. Place in your fermenting bin. Add water, and let cool. Add crushed Campden tablets. Add raisins and cinnamon stick, if using. Let it sit for three days, stirring frequently.
Strain and discard flowers. Add orange and lemon juice and grated rind. Stir in sugar and nutrients. The specific gravity should be between 1.100 and 1.110. Sprinkle yeast over the mixture and stir. Stir daily for three or four days, until frothing stops.
Strain the wine. Siphon into your demijon and place airlock.

For a dry wine, rack in three weeks, and every three months for one year. Then bottle.

For a sweet wine, rack at three weeks. Add 1/2 cup sugar dissolved in 1 cup wine. Stir gently, and place back into your demijon Repeat this process every six weeks until fermentation does not restart with the addition of sugar. Rack it every three months until one year old then bottle. This wine is best if you can refrain from drinking it for two full years from the date it was started. It will definitely improve with age.

The calyces, along with the white sap, will make the wine bitter and require many years to age. Be sure not to get any in the wine. The best source of dandelions is your own or a friends yard. That way, you can be sure when the lawn was last treated -- with either fertilizer or herbicide. Dandelions bloom in early spring, so it should be no problem to harvest them before trying to eliminate them.

ELDERBERRY WINE

4 1/2 cups Elderberries
12 cups water
5 3/4 cups sugar
1 Lemon, juice only
3 Campden tablets
1 teaspoon pectic enzyme
1 teaspoon yeast nutrients
1 package wine yeast

Wash the berries and remove stalks. Crush and place the in your fermenting bin. Dissolve Campden tablets in 2 cups hot water. Add this to the fermenting bin. Stir in lemon juice and pectic enzyme then leave overnight.
Add 10 cups water and yeast let it sit for 3 days, stirring daily. Make sure the fruit stays submerged.
On day 4, strain out the fruit. Add the sugar and nutrients. Place in to the demijon and attach an airlock.

For a dry wine, rack in three weeks and return to the demijon. Rack again in three months, and every three months until 1 year old then bottle.

For a sweet wine, rack at three weeks. Add 1/2 cup sugar dissolved in 1 cup wine. Stir gently, and place back into the demijon. Repeat this process every six weeks until fermentation does not restart with the addition of sugar. Rack it every three months until one year old then bottle.

GINGER WINE

1/4 cup dried Ginger (not powdered)
2 Campden tablets
1 cup Raisins
2 Oranges (rind and juice)
2 Lemons (rind and juice)
2 Campden tablets
7 cups brown sugar (Demerara)
1 tsp nutrients
Yeast
Water

Simmer ginger, raisins and thinly peeled orange and lemon zest in 4 cups water for 15 minutes. Strain the liquid into the fermenting bin. Put the solids back into saucepan and add another 4 cups of water. Simmer again for 15 minutes and strain into fermenting bin. Simmer solids in 4 cups water one more time, and strain.

Add the juice of oranges and lemons, Campden tablets, sugar and nutrients to in to the fermenting bin. Stir until the sugar is dissolved. Add water to make up to 1 gallon then let sit overnight. Add the yeast. The next day

Stir the mixture daily for 5 to 6 days or until specific gravity is 1.040. Siphon into the demijon and add an airlock.

For a dry wine, rack in six weeks, then every three months for one year then bottle.

For a sweet wine, rack at six weeks. Add 1/2 cup sugar dissolved in 1 cup wine. Stir gently, and place back into the demijon. Repeat process every six weeks until fermentation does not restart with the addition of sugar. Rack it every three months until one year old.

Wine is ready to drink one year after the date the batch was started.

Bottle the wine when you are sure it is stable.

MEAD
3 pounds Honey
2 tablespoon acid blend
1 teaspoon nutrients
2 Campden tablets
1/2 teaspoon tannin /a tea bag
1 package champagne/wine yeast
Water

Dissolve the honey in 1/2 gallon of warm water with nutrients, acid and tannin. Add cold water to make up to 1 gallon. Add crushed Campden tablets. Let it sit overnight. The specific gravity should be 1.100. Add yeast and place in a demijon. Rack when Specific Gravity reaches 1.020. Rack again when Specific Gravity reaches 1.010. Continue to rack every 3 months for 1 year.
This method will yield a dry mead. For sweeter mead, add 1/2 cup of honey dissolved in 1 cup of mead. Rack every 6 weeks, adding more honey, until fermentation has ceased. Then rack every 3 months for 1 year with no further honey additions.
Bottle the wine when you are sure it is stable.
The nature of honey makes this wine require frequent racking. A very fine sediment will accumulate in the bottle if

it sits for more than a few months before drinking. This may be minimized if the following steps are taken:
Boil the honey in some water in a large pot -- it will boil up quite high. Allow it to simmer while skimming the foam off the top. Continue until it no longer forms any foam.
If adding honey for a sweet wine, boil 1/2 cup honey with 1 cup water instead of in some of the mead. Skim as above. Allow to cool completely before putting it into the mead.

NETTLE WINE
8 cups Nettle tops
1 pound Raisins
6 1/2 cups granulated sugar
1 teaspoon yeast nutrients
2 Lemons (or Oranges)
2 Campden tablets
1 gallon water
1 package wine yeast

Pick tender nettle tops in the spring. Rinse well. Simmer in water with lemon (or orange) rind for 20 minutes. Strain the liquid into a fermenting bin and squeeze all liquid out of the pulp then discard the pulp. Add water to make up to 1 gallon. Add sugar, nutrients, lemon (or orange) juice, raisins and Campden tablets. Stir to dissolve sugar the n let it sit overnight.

Next day the specific gravity should be 1.090 - 1.100. Stir in the yeast. Stir daily for 2 or 3 days until frothing ceases. Siphon this into the demijon and attach airlock. For a dry wine, rack in six weeks, and every three months for one year. Then bottle.

For a sweet wine, rack at six weeks. Add 1/2 cup sugar dissolved in 1 cup of wine. Stir gently and place back into the demijon. Repeat this process every six weeks until the fermentation does not restart with the addition of sugar. Rack every three months until one year old then bottle it.

The wine is best if you can refrain from drinking it for one full year from the date it was started.

Herb guide

"Everything on this earth has a purpose, every disease a herb to cure it"

As you can see from the herb list below, this is just a selection of the aliments that can be treated with a few simple herbs, neither the list below, nor the recipes above are exhaustive, they simply provided you with a taster of what can be done, I want you to get an understanding of what herbs will treat what ailments, and what works best for you. Then you can start to test some of your own recipes for yourself, you can begin to further your own understanding of herbalism and create your own tea recipes.

AGRIMONY

Botanical Name: Agrimonia Eupatoria

Plant Family: Rosaceae

Plant description: Agrimonies have one to two foot branchy stems covered with a fine, silky down and terminate in spikes of yellow flowers. Both the flowers and the notched leaves give off a faint characteristic lemony scent when crushed. After the flowers fade they give place to tiny clinging "burrs" which will quickly adhere to your clothing if you brush by an it plant in a hedgerow.

Part used: The flower, the leave and the stem

Harvest: Just before and just after the flowering period.

ALOE VERA

Botanical Name: Aloe Vera Barbadensis

Plant Family: Asphodelaceae

Plant description: Aloe Vera is a stem less or very short-stemmed succulent plant. The leaves are thick and fleshy, green to grey-green, with some varieties showing white flecks on the upper and lower stem surfaces. The margin of the leaf is serrated and has small white teeth.

Part used: The succulent leaf stems

Harvest: anytime during the growing period.

ANGELICA

Botanical Name: Angelica Archangelica

Plant Family: Umbelliferae

Plant description: Angelica has a thick, hollow stem and long-stalked, deeply divided leaves; they have tiny green-white flowers in late summer, followed by ovate ridged seeds

Part used: All parts for different uses

Harvest: Leaves during the early growing season, flowers in mid summer and seed s toward early autumn.

ANISE

Botanical Name: Pimpinella Anisum L.

Plant Family: Umbelliferae

Plant Description: Anise has feathery leaves and flat, white flower heads, followed by fruit and then small, aromatic brown seeds, with a distinctive liquorice taste.

Parts Used: seeds

Harvest: cut the leave to use fresh as you need to, take the seed head when still just green and dry them, make sure all is harvested before the first frost in autumn.

ARNICA

Botanical Name: Arnica Montana

Plant Family: Asteraceae

Plant description: Grows up to 2 feet with orange flowers not dissimilar to daisies. The stems are round and hairy, terminating with up to 3 flower stalks, the flowers are approximately 3 inches across. The leaves are vibrant green. The upper leaves are toothed and slightly hairy, while lower leaves have rounded tips.

Part used: The flower heads

Harvest: during the flowering period.

BASIL

Botanical Name: Ocimum Basilicum

Plant Family: Lamiaceae

Plant description: The rich distinct scent of a basil leaf makes the identification of this medicinal plant certain. Basil consists of one upright quadrangular stem branching on all sides with two dark green leaves at every node. Whorls of small white flowers appear toward the end of the growing season.

Part used: Leaf

Harvest: Harvest the leaf during the growing season.

BAY

Botanical Name: Laurus Noblis

Plant Family: Lauraceae

Plant description: The bay is a tree with aromatic, evergreen leaves and shiny gray bark. The tree is normally around 3 to 6 feet talk in the UK. The leaves are oval, 3 to 4 inches long quite thick and leathery.

Part used: The leaves

Harvest: all year round.

BIRCH

Botanical Name: Betula Pendula

Plant Family: Betulaceae

Plant description: The silver birch is a very common tree in Britain, and is very easy to identify, the bark is whitish in colour and shed layers like crisp paper, their branches are thin and whip like, with a smooth brown bark, the leaves are small and roughly triangular with toothed edges.

Part used: The sap

Harvest: just as the leaves begin to show in the latter part of March or first part of April.

BERGAMOT

Botanical Name: Monarda Didyma

Plant Family: Lamiaceae

Plant description: Bergamot can be up to 3 feet high. It has quite erect stalks. The lightly toothed leaves are opposite each other on the stalks, a bluish green that can be tinged red. It produces large red purple flower heads.

Part used: Leaf and flowers.

Harvest: just before or during the flowering season.

BLACKBERRY

Botanical Name: Rubus sp.

Plant Family: Rosaceae

Plant description: the thorny canes can spring up anywhere they are very resilient with oval toothed leaves approximately 3 to 4 inches long. The flowers are 5 petalled, usually white with a touch of pink. The fruit is roughly conical approximately 1 to 11/2 inches long, and bulbous comprised of clusters of single dark purple berries

Part used: The berries

Harvest: late summer, as late as possible.

BLUEBERRY

Botanical Name: Vaccinium sp.

Plant Family: Ericaceae

Plant description: The leaves are small and elliptical, up to a quarter of an inch long.
The flowers are bell shaped and hang in rows with white petals.
The fruits are a dark purple with a whitish bloom on the skin. The plant can grow up to twelve feet in height.

Part used: The fruits

Harvest: Early autumn when the fruits are ripe.

BURDOCK

Botanical Name: Arctium Lappa

Plant Family: Asteraceae

Plant description: burdock is a common plant with sticky burrs that will attach to your clothing. It grows up to four feet and has purple flowers that bloom throughout the summer and in to autumn. The leaves are small and heart shaped, with green tops and whitish undersides.

Part used: The roots

Harvest: Anytime.

CALENDULA

Botanical Name: Calendula Officinalis

Plant Family: Asteraceae

Plant description: Calendula will grow up to three feet tall, producing lots of dandelion like flowers of bright yellow and orange. The leaves are oval and bright green sprouting from the stem.

Part used: Flower heads and petals

Harvest: during the summer season.

CARAWAY

Botanical Name: Carum Carvi

Plant Family: Apiaceae

Plant description: Caraway bi-annual growing up to two feet high. Its leaves are feathery like that of the carrot, but have a tendency to droop lower. The flowers appear in umbelllifer groups and are small, white with pink tinges. The seeds when they appear are pointedly oval and are dark brown. The seed cases appear on the stem of the plant.

Part used: Seeds

Harvest: Late Autumn.

CHAMOMILE

Botanical Name: Matricaria Recutita

Plant Family: Asteraceae

Plant description: German chamomile grows wild in Europe and other temperate regions. It is an annual growing to 1 m with erect branching stems. The leaves are mildly aromatic, pinnate with fine filiform segments. The simple daisy-like flowers are sweetly perfumed with white petals and yellow centres.

Part used: The flower

Harvest: Collection between late spring and late summer.

CHERRY (WILD)

Botanical Name: Prunus Serotina

Plant Family: Rosaceae

Plant description: The wild cherry tree has very distinctive purple brown bark with horizontal markings; the papery bark of this tree can be pealed to reveal bright red bark underneath. The leaves are oval with serrated edges about the length of your palm. In spring it will flower in clusters with small groups of white-pink flowers, which create stalked cherries in late summer to early autumn.

Part used: Fruits

Harvest: Early autumn.

CHICKWEED

Botanical Name: Stellaria Media

Plant Family: Caryophyllaceae

Plant description: a short plant usually less than six inches tall they form beds of plants along the floor. They have small oval pointed leaves which grow opposite each other and the stem has fine hair running its length.

The Chickweed has tiny white flowers which are five petallaled but deeply cut so it looks like ten.

Part used: The whole plant

Harvest: During growing season.

CINNAMON

Botanical Name: Cinnamomum Zeylanicum

Plant Family: Lauraceae

Plant description: The Cinnamon tree is a small evergreen tree, not native to the UK. The bark is widely used as a spice due to its colour and odour. The leaves are slightly longer than six inches and oval the greenish flowers have a distinctive odour. It is a fruiting tree producing a small purple berry, usually not larger than half an inch. Unless you're in Sri Lanka or parts of southern India, you are unlikely to find this tree growing wild.

Part used: The bark

Harvest: Anytime

CITRONELLA

Botanical Name: Cymbopogon Nardus

Plant Family: Poaceae/Gramineae

Plant description: The Citronella is an aromatic grass grown in Sri Lanka, its flowers appear in spikes and the stems of the plant can be mistaken for sugar cane. The leaves (blades of grass) are drooping and shaped as a lance

Again, as Citronella is not native to the UK, you are unlikely to encounter it while foraging,

Part used: The leaves

Harvest: Anytime.

COLTSFOOT

Botanical Name: Tussilago Farfara

Plant Family: Asteraceae

Plant description: Coltsfoot has long, hoof like leaves, usually not longer than four inches across with angular teeth around the edges. The top and the bottom of young leaves are covered in fine woolly like hairs. They produce small yellow dandelion like flowers through the summer season

Part used: All the plant

Harvest: Late summer.

COMFREY

Botanical Name: Symphytum Officinale

Plant Family: Boraginaceae

Plant description: The Comfrey has a thick stem compared to other plants, is quite hairy, and can grow up to five feet tall. It produces flowers in clusters which can be blue, purple or off white. The oblong leaves are not uniform and will change shape depending on where they are on the stem, the lower leaves being broad at the base
Part used: The leaves and the root

Harvest: Late summer.

DANDELION

Botanical Name: Taraxacum Officinale

Plant Family: Asteraceae

Plant description: The dandelion is an easy to spot plant; it has a hollow leafless stem, between four and six inches high the leaves are a deep green and coarsely toothed sprouting from the base of the plant. Each stem has a single large bright yellow flower with many thin petals in early summer, with a large white feathered seed head from mid summer.

Part used: The leaves and the root

Harvest: Leaves in spring before the flowers appear, roots in the autumn.

ECHINACEA

Botanical Name: Echinacea Purpurea

Plant Family: Asteracea

Plant description: Plant description: Echinacea has a long stout hand bristly stalk up to three feet in height. The leaves are thin land lance like up to eight inches long; the pink flowers are large, up to three inches in diameter and there is usually only one per stalk. The flower has a cone in the centre which is spiky and purple brown in colour.

Part used: All of the plant

Harvest: during the flowering season.

ELDER

Botanical Name: Sambuccus Nigra

Plant Family: Caprifoliaceae

Plant description: A common tree of the UK the elder has mid to dark pointed oval leaves growing five to a stalk. The bark is a very pale colour with a warty texture and the branches are hollow with white pith in the middle. In early spring umbellifer groups of white flowers form on stalks which transform in to clusters of sweet tasting berries.

Part used: The flowers and fruits

Harvest: collect some of the flowers in early spring and the fruits in late summer.

EUCALPTUS

Botanical Name: Eucalyptus Globulus

Plant Family: Myrtaceae

Plant description: Eucalyptus is a very tall tree, reaching upwards of fifteen meters. In very harsh and exposed conditions it can adopt a shrubby habit. The tree has rough grey bark which shed from the top down but not all the way down the trunk of the tree. White flowers form on the tree from winter through to early summer followed by they grey fruits.

Eucalyptus is not native to the UK and you are unlikely to find one while foraging.

Part used: The leaves

Harvest: During the early summer season.

FENNEL

Botanical Name: Foeniculum Vulgare.

Plant Family: Apiaceae

Plant description: The Fennel plant is native to Southern Europe and Western Asia. It is an aromatic perennial with thick blue green pith filled stems. The feathery leaves are alternate, deeply divided into thread like segments with strong aniseed like aroma. It has umbels of small ycllow flowers which ripen into small oval shaped, grey brown seeds.

Part used: The seed

Harvest: Collected in autumn and shaken to release seeds when dried.

FEVERFEW

Botanical Name: Tanacetum Parthenium

Plant Family: Asteraceae

Plant description: A native of Southeast Europe, feverfew is a much branched woody perennial growing up to 1 meter. The leaves are strongly scented, light green, feathery, pinnate or bi-pinnate. The many flower heads have white petals and yellow centres and occur throughout summer.

Part used: Leaf and flower

Harvest: When plant is coming into flower.

GINGER

Botanical Name: Zingiber Officinale

Plant Family: Zingiberareae

Plant description: Native to Asia this aromatic, perennial herb grows to 60 cm in height with narrow lanceolate leaves on green stems. The flowering stalk arises from the root and ends in a spike from which white or yellow flower blooms. Ginger has been a prized plant since the earliest times. It is regarded as one of the world's best medicines.

Part used: The root

Harvest: The root is dug after at least one year of growth.

GOLDENSEAL

Botanical Name: Hydrastis Canadensis

Plant Family: N.O. Ranunculaceae

Plant description:goldenseal grows to around a foot in height, branching near the top. The leaves are lobed and can be up to 6 inches in diameter. The green-white flower of the goldenseal arrives in early spring and gives way to a large berrylike head which turns bright red in autumn. The rootstock is a bright yellow colour.

Part used: root & rhizome

Harvest: only harvest a small section of root after the main growing season (late summer/ early autumn) other wise the plant may die.

HAWTHORN BERRY

Botanical Name: Crataegus Monogyna

Plant Family: Rosaceae

Plant description: Native to Europe, North Africa and West Asia, Hawthorn is an erect shrub or small tree to 9 m but more commonly 4–6 m. It has many spreading branches with thorns 5–25 mm long. The leaves are alternate and mostly ovate, deeply lobed and toothed at the tips 15–50 mm long. Flowers are white or pink with 5 petals in clusters at the ends of the branches and branchlets, with a strong scent. The fruit is a small berry which becomes red as it ripens with a yellowish flesh.

Part used: Leaf and flower, and berry

Harvest: The leaf and flower should be harvested when the flowers are mostly open but before they begin to fade.

HOPS

Botanical Name: Humulus Lupulus

Plant Family: Cannabaceae

Plant description: Hops is a climbing English native. Hops stems can be as long as twenty two feet long with deep green heart shaped leaves with finely toothed edges. The flowers of the female plant are the ones harvested and are called strobiles; they resemble small pine cones up to two inches long and are whitish yellow in colour.

Part used: The flowers

Harvest: Mid to late summer.

HOREHOUND

Botanical Name: Marrubium Vulgare

Plant Family: Lamiaceae

Plant description: Horehound is a very bushy plant which sends up many square shaped downy stems growing to around a foot and a half in height. The greyish leaves tend to be wrinkled and are quite rough to the touch on top but downy texture on the underside. Horehound flowers are white and form in clusters on the top part of the main stem.

Part used: The leaves and young shoots

Harvest: during the growing season.

JUNIPER

Botanical Name: Juniperus

Plant Family: Cupressaceae

Plant description: The Juniper is a bush of the pine family, growing as tall as twenty five feet tall it is common in mountainous regions of Europe and Asia. Rather than leaves it has stiff needles up to half an inch long and it is the female of the species which produces the small cone which in turn create the blue black berries which can take as long as three years to mature.

Part used: The fruit

Harvest: late summer.

LAVENDER

Botanical Name: Lavendula Augustifolia

Plant Family: Lamiaceae

Plant description: Lavender a native of mountainous regions of the Western Mediterranean countries. This English Lavender is a woody perennial growing to about 80cm. The leaves are opposite, narrow lanceolate or oblong linear, grey to green covered in fine hairs. Flowers are purple, but can be white, grey blue, pink or dark purple, tubular in loose spikes. The English lavender can be distinguished from other Lavenders by its long narrow, smooth edged leaves.

Other species have leaves which are toothed or frilled or shorter.

Part used: Flower

Harvest: The flower should be harvested when the plant is in its early flowering stage.

LEMON

Botanical Name: Citrus Limonium

Plant Family: Rutaceae

Plant description: The lemon tree can grow as high as twenty feet and has thorny twigs, the mature leaves are dark green on top and lighter underneath usually between two and four inches long and finely toothed along the edges. During early spring like most fruiting trees it produces a whitish pink blossom. Whilst found these days in most hot countries the Lemon tree is not native to the UK and you are very unlikely to find one while foraging, unless you are in a hotter country.

Part used: The fruit

Harvest: late summer to early autumn.

LEMON BALM

Botanical Name: Melissa Officinalis

Plant Family: Lamiaceae

Plant description: Lemon Balm or Melissa Balm as it is known as has slightly hairy square stems growing 30–80 cm high. The leaves are opposite, ovate, light green, lightly toothed with a lemon scent. Flowers are whitish, occasionally pink or yellow in small clusters in the axils of the upper leaves.

Part used: Leaf

Harvest: The leaf should be harvested when the plant is coming into flower.

LEMON VERBENA

Botanical Name: Aloysia Triphylla

Plant Family: Verbenaceae

Plant description: Verbena is a very unassuming plant which can grow higher than six feet; it has a woody stem with light green, highly fragrant, pointed leaves and small pale purple flowers branching from the stem toward late summer.

Part used: The leaves

Harvest: Anytime during summer.

LIQUORICE

Botanical Name: Glycyrrhiza Glabra

Plant Family: Fabaceae

Plant description: Native to Southern Europe to Pakistan, liquorice likes hot summers and will grow to 1.5 m. The pinnate leaves with 4–7 pairs of ovate leaflets, 25–50 mm long. The flowers are arranged in loose racemes of 20–30 flowers 10 mm long in the axils of the leaves. These form separate pods 10–25 mm long. The roots and rhizomes are yellow brown inside and can grow to 8 m long. They have a strong sweet flavour. It takes three years before the plants can be harvested.

Part used: The root

Harvest: The root is collected in autumn, winter or early spring.

MALLOW

Botanical Name: Althaea Officinalis

Plant Family: Malvaceae

Plant description: The Mallow has quite fleshy stems and grows on upright storks between three and four feet. It has round lobed leaves with uneven toothed margins and a soft down covers the leaves and storks. During summer the Mallow produces a profusion of pinkish flowers with five petals.

Part used: The leaves and roots

Harvest: During the growing season.

MEADOWSWEET

Botanical Name: Filipendula Ulmaria

Plant Family: Rosaceae

Plant description: Meadowsweet is a very tall plant growing upwards of three feet in height. It flowers during the summer season forming clumps of sweet smelling white flowers. The leaves are composite leaflets which are two coloured, being green on top and silver on the underside. The meadowsweet is most common on boggy ground.

Part used: The flowers

Harvest: Anytime.

MINT

Botanical Name: Mentha Spicata

Plant Family: Lamiaceae

Plant description: The common mint can be found throughout Europe, it will grow around one foot tall from many green stems. The leaves, coming from the stems are a mid green in colour, up to three inches in length and growing opposite each other on the stem and are slightly toothed along the edges. They smell strongly of mint when brushed against or rubbed.

Part used: The aerial section of the plant

Harvest: Anytime.

MUGWORT

Botanical Name: Artemisia Vulgaris

Plant Family: Asteraceae

Plant description: Mugwort is an herb with a long history of uses in both traditional Western and Chinese medicine. It is used in magic and ceremonial practices. Mugwort grows to 1.8 m tall. The undersides of the leaves are downy and whitish, green above, pinnate or bi-pinnate with toothed leaflets. The brownish yellow to red flowers, are many and small, arranged in panicles towards the top of the plant.

Part used: Leaf and flower

Harvest: The leaf should be harvested when the plant comes into flower.

MULLEIN

Botanical Name: Verbascum Thapsus

Plant Family: Scrophulariaceae

Plant description: A very tall single stalk bi yearly herb that can grow up to seven feet tall. The texture of the plant is downy and soft, it's leaves are long and thin, up to twelve inches long. The mullein flowers are yellow and form densely on a club like spike during summer.

Part used: The leaves and flowers

Harvest: harvest only from plants more than one season old, and not so much as to kill the plant.

NETTLE

Botanical Name: Urtica Dioica

Plant Family: Urticaceae

Plant description: The common Nettle is much maligned as a weed, but this hairy plant with its heavily toothed leaves has many great uses. It can grow as high as 3 feet and the leaves which grow opposite from the main stalk have many toxic hairs which if get under she skin can cause rashes.

Part used: Leaf

Harvest: During the growing season

PEPPERMINT

Botanical Name: Mentha Piperita

Plant Family: Lamiaceae

Plant description: Like most mints, the peppermint grows up to three feet in height, it's leaves grow opposite each other, are around two inches in length and are toothed at the edges. The peppermint branches from the rootstock in to several stems and is very fragrant to the touch.

Part used: Leaf

Harvest: the leaves should be collected before the plant comes in to flower during late summer.

PURSLANE

Botanical Name: Portulaca Oleracea

Plant Family: Portulacaceae

Plant description: This quick growing plant will grow just over one foot high, the red reddish stem producing thick, egg shaped leaves. During the summer season Purslane creates pastel yellow-orange flowers between the leaves.

Part used: The leaves

Harvest: During the growing season.

RASPBERRY

Botanical Name: Rubus Idaeus

Plant Family: Rosaceae

Plant description: Raspberry is native to Europe and Asia and grows to 2 m. It has small sharp bristles on its stem green above with furrowed veins and light creamy grey underneath with 3 or 5 ovate leaflets. The white flowers are in drooping branchlets and the fleshy cone shaped fruit are red to yellow and delicious.

Part used: Leaf

Harvest: The plant should be harvested just before flowering.

ROSEMARY

Botanical Name: Rosemarinus Officinalis.

Plant Family: Lamiaceae

Plant description: This bushy plant can grow as high as four to six feet branching from a woody stem. The woody branches have a rough mid brown flaky bark and lance like leaves around an inch long which are dark on top and paler on the underside. Rosemary is a very fragrant plant when brushed against.

Part used: The leaves

Harvest: During the growing season.

SAGE

Botanical Name: Salvia Officinalis

Plant Family: Lamiaceae

Plant description: Sage is native to Southern Europe,
particularly near the Mediterranean. It is a small, upright,
woody stemmed shrub to 70 cm tall. The young green stems
are square white and woolly. The grey-green leaves are
aromatic opposite ovate to lanceolate, with rough surfaces.
Flowers are bluish-purple in terminal spikes. It is a semi-
deciduous perennial.

Part used: Leaf and flower

Harvest: As the plant comes into flower.

SANDALWOOD

Botanical Name: Santalum Album

Plant Family: Santalaceae

Plant description: The Sandalwood, a native of India is a small parasitic evergreen tree around twenty feet high. The branches have smooth gray bark and grow opposite each other drooping downward. The leaves are smooth and oval; the bark is a light yellow colour and splits easily.

This is not a native of the UK and unless you are in India you are unlikely to find this tree while foraging.

Part used: The bark, powdered

Harvest: Anytime.

SLIPPERY ELM

Botanical Name: Ulmus Rubra

Plant Family: Ulmaceae

Plant description: This medium sized tree is generally found only in North America. In it's native environment it can be as tall as fifty feet in height and has an open crown of spreading branches. The branches have a reddish brown bark which tends to grow downward like the Willow; the trunk tends to have fissures and something of a gummy feel to it as well as a subtle but distinct odour. The Slippery elm has long leaves which tend to darken as autumn approaches

Unfortunately, as this tree is not native to the UK, you are unlikely to find this while foraging unless you are in it's country of origin.

Part used: The inner bark, powdered

Harvest: Anytime.

SOAP WORT

Botanical Name: Saponaria Officinalis

Plant Family: Caryophyllaceae

Plant description: Soapwort is a fairly common herb which grows a single stem to around two feet in height. The soapwort will usually grow in bunches and the leave, which are generally oval grow opposite each other on the stem. During early summer it will begin to produce small flowers with five petals, ranging between a whitish pink to a full rose colour at the end of the stem in groups.

Part used: the flower in the summer, the root in autumn

Harvest: As above.

SPEARMINT

Botanical Name: Mentha Spicata

Plant Family: Lamiaceae

Plant description: Spearmint is an invasive plant growing up to three feet in height. It has greyish green leaves which are highly aromatic of mint to the touch and created spikes of purple flowers in tiered groups.

Part used: The leaf

Harvest: Anytime during the growing season.

ST. JOHNS WORT

Botanical Name: Hypericum Perforatum

Plant Family: Clusiaceae

Plant description: St. John's Wort is a very hardy plant, growing up to two and a half feet high, during late spring and early summer it is covered in very fragrant five petalled small yellow flowers with clusters for golden stamens. These are accompanied by small deep green long thin leaves.

Part used: petals and leaves

Harvest: mid spring when the flowers are fully open but before the mid day heat.

TEA TREE

Botanical Name: Melaleuca Alternifolia

Plant Family: Myrtaceae

Plant description: The Tea Tree can grow as high as twenty feet tall spreading to thirteen feet. The bark of this scrubby bush is quite papery composed of several layers. It has small narrow pointed leaves and small white flowers which form up in spring.

Unfortunately, the Tea Tree is a native is Australia and it is very unlikely (unless you are in that country) that you will find it while foraging.

Part used: The leaves

Harvest: Late spring to early summer.

THYME

Botanical Name: Thymus Vulgaris

Plant Family: Lamiaceae

Plant description: Thyme is a native to the Western Mediterranean and Southern Italy. Thyme is a small woody stemmed shrub, densely branched and sometimes gnarled and twisted. It grows to 30 cm tall with opposite, grey-green, aromatic, linear to elliptic leaves. The small flowers are white to lilac in many-flowered terminal inflorescences. Thyme retains most of its leaves in winter. There are many different cultivars and varieties of thyme that differ widely in leaf colour and flavour.

Part used: Leaf

Harvest As the plant comes into flower.

VALERIAN

Botanical Name: Valeriana Officinalis

Plant Family: Valerianaceae

Plant description: Valerian is native to Europe and Western Asia. It grows to 1.8 m high with grooved, hollow flower stems bearing small white or pink flowers in terminal inflorescences. The leaves are pinnate with lanceolate leaflets. The plant forms a dense crown from which fine, matted, strongly aromatic roots grow.

Part used: Root

Harvest: In late autumn to winter when the tops have died down.

VIOLET

Botanical Name: Viola Riviniana

Plant Family: Violaceae

Plant description: The Violet is a very common wildflower with heart shaped leaves they grow in all directions from the stem, and then form deep purple flowers with a pale spur.

Part used: The petals

Harvest: Late spring to early summer.

WILLOW

Botanical Name: Salix Alba

Plant Family: Salicaceae

Plant description: This beautiful tree prefers to root near streams and rivers and can grow as large as seventy five feet. In early spring the slender branches produce very small yellow flowers followed by long thin leaves which are smooth and a green-beige colour. The tree usually has many branches overhanging ponds and streams, like a woman dipping her head in to the water.

Part used: the bark of the young branches

Harvest: mid spring.

WITCH HAZEL

Botanical Name: Hamamelis Virginiana

Plant Family: Hamamelidaceae

Plant description: The Witch Hazel is a late flowering shrub. Like the Elder it produces many crooked branches from one root, which can be up to six inches in diameter and as long as twelve feet in length and has a smooth grey bark.

Part used: Bark, extreme care must be taken, if taken orally can result in nausea and liver damage, never take more than one gram per day.

Harvest: Anytime.

YARROW

Botanical Name: Achillea Millefolium

Plant Family: Asteraceae

Plant description: Yarrow has flower stems growing to 70 cm. The bipinnate leaves are very finely divided. The flowers are white to light pink, composite in dense terminal umbels.

Part used: Leaf and flower

Harvest: When the plant is flowering, while the flowers are young.